Dragonfly Games

Developing and Supporting Dyslexic Learners 7–14

SALLY RAYMOND

 David Fulton Publishers

David Fulton Publishers
2 Park Square, Milton Park, Abingdon, Oxon OX14 4RN

270 Madison Avenue, New York, NY 10016

David Fulton Publishers is an imprint of the Taylor & Francis Group, an informa business

First published in Great Britain by David Fulton Publishers 2003
Transferred to digital printing

British Library Cataloguing in Publication Data
A catalogue record for this book is available from the British Library.

ISBN 1-84312-038-0

Illustrations by Jane Bottomley
Typeset by FiSH Books, London

Contents

Introduction

About this book

Dragonfly Games have been designed to support and develop the dyslexic learning profile through the use of games. By utilising the achievable, repetitive and enjoyable aspects of game-play, specific barriers to learning are overcome and success is achieved through the use of experience, over-learning and discovery.

As well as delivering specific topics of learning, such as spelling patterns, word decoding and comprehension skills, Dragonfly Games encourage dyslexic pupils to master skills beyond those of literacy and numeracy development. Structured targets evoke thinking skills and tactical strategies. The application of rules encourages amiable and just social interaction, providing lessons in sportsmanship and the experience of winning and losing in a competitive environment, but one that lacks many of the factors that often precipitate failure and demoralisation.

This is an important aspect of Dragonfly Games. Many dyslexic pupils are only too familiar with failure, and can easily become anxious and reluctant to participate in activities that rely on application speed or proficiency of skill for success. Dragonfly Games are heavily loaded with luck. The throw of a die, or turn of a card, can make all the difference to the winning outcome, luring players into participation and encouraging the desire to repeat application in the hope of success. This approach enables players to experience winning and failing in a 'safe' environment, increasing their confidence and ability to face the challenges and unknowns occurring elsewhere in their lives.

Teachers can choose games that focus on a specific topic of learning and/or facilitate access to specific application and delivery techniques. Games can be adapted to suit the age and need of players, and many can be usefully and enjoyably employed to meet the learning needs of non-dyslexic pupils too.

Laminated games can provide wet-playtime activities. Games can (and should) be used for the learning, revision and consolidation of inputs delivered in class, but exercised at home alongside parents etc., involving all parties in the 'little, often' application style that suits the learning needs of dyslexic pupils. Pupils can also be encouraged to devise their own games, developing their ability to use varied methods of application that are useful for overcoming weaknesses within their own learning profile. This can help them to identify and employ practical and supportive study-skill techniques, reducing the frustrations and impact of failure, and increasing the ability to employ autonomous application with success.

Why does playing games support the dyslexic learning profile?

Dyslexia is not a unitary condition. Dyslexics can possess learning profiles that vary significantly between individuals. Specific learning weaknesses (and strengths), harboured primarily within the audio, visual, semantic and kinaesthetic modalities of the brain, affect the learning needs and styles of dyslexic pupils according to the degree to which they arrest assimilation of teaching inputs, and the extent to which teaching inputs are adapted to reduce the impact of barriers to learning.

Games commonly consist of structured activities repetitively applied in a manner that results in a variety of outcomes. The repetitive nature of game-play delivers application and experience through a 'little, often' approach, increasing the opportunity for learning to take place. As familiarity and confidence grow, the working (short-term) memory becomes experienced in handling different aspects of each game, encouraging successful transferral of learning into long-term memory and the opportunity for further discovery. By reducing the demands on working memory in this way, specific processing difficulties face less interference from input overload, again increasing the opportunity for understanding and success.

Game A
Quiz the Words

A game developing spelling skills

When spelling a word, it must be transformed into an appropriate sequence of letters sourced from a lexicon of knowledge stored in the long-term memory. This task is made harder by the numerous rules and riddles of the English language, and by the difficulties dyslexic learners face in establishing secure and retrievable memory traces.

English spellings contain audio and visual elements. It is not uncommon for dyslexics to have weaknesses within both of these modalities. Others will experience a singular weakness. These factors both reduce the development of learning through assimilation and experience, and lead to compensatory over-reliance on alternative approaches to spelling. It is therefore important to integrate both the visual and audio features of letter groupings, and to explore the meaningful (semantic) employment of different letter-to-sound combinations in different words.

Preparation

Copy templates on to coloured card and laminate for longevity. Cut up and label the backs of cards 'letter pattern' or 'question master' and store in a labelled envelope. Add a copy of the playing instructions. Introduce and play alongside pupils, then provide blank score cards for further play.

New letter groups can be added to revise and over-learn spelling and reading inputs.

Players can be challenged to combine two letter patterns into a word if they can. Invented words are allowed, as long as their spelling matches pronunciation.

Questions and tasks can be altered according to need.

Game A
Quiz the Words

Name: ....

Date: ....Form: ....

Playing instructions

Place letter group cards face down on the table.

Turn over a letter group card.

Write down a word containing that letter group.

Then turn over a question master card.

If your word scores a 'yes', or if it can be used to complete a task successfully, score five points.

Errors (e.g. spelling 'kite' as 'kight') are awarded two points for matching audio with letters, but are disallowed from being entered into the quiz.

Example scorecard

Word	Score (relating to question master card)	Word	Score
happy	0 (not invented word)		
rane	2 (misspelling that matches sound)		
delight	5 (more than six letters)		
shop	5 (can be used as a noun)		

© Sally Raymond, 2003, 'Dragonfly Games', ISBN 1-84312-038-0. Published by David Fulton Publishers.

Game A
Quiz the Words

Letter group cards

igh	all	fl	str	ai	ar	ck	kn
tch	ph	ance	ing	thr	ow	ly	pl
ou	sh	es	ee	br	I	and	tion

Game A
Quiz the Words

Question master cards

Does the word have an opposite? e.g. hot/cold	Write four words that rhyme with the word (+2 if spellings are correct)	Does the word contain more than two vowels?	Use the word in a story with a happy ending
Add one or more letters to the end of the word to make a new word	Can you make a new word by removing one letter (you may rearrange letters if you need to)	Write two words that might follow your word, e.g. rain *cloud*, rain *drop*	Can the word be used as a noun?
Is the word invented?	Devise a crossword clue for the word	Hide the word from sight, spell aloud, backwards	Write down a sentence using the word twice

Game B
Sounds of a Picture

A game for audio memory

This game prompts audio memory to recall sounds attached to a visual image. English spellings rely greatly on this integration of visual and audio memories in order to match phonics with display. In order to spell 'kite' and 'night' correctly, not only must the 'ite' and 'ight' patterns be associated with the sound, but visual discrimination is required so that the appropriate spelling choice is made.

When one is reading, visual and audio memory traces combine (along with word meanings) to achieve decoding success. 'Sounds of a picture' move these processing skills away from the written word, developing audio memory skills in a context that is challenging and different.

Thinking skills are also developed, along with experience and practice in applying descriptive language to capture the essence of different sounds.

Preparation

Collect a variety of pictures, such as postcards of the seaside, rural and urban locations, photographs of different events and activities, historical pictures displaying action and a variety of background settings.

This game involves the players identifying the **sounds** they might hear if they were the cameraman/artist, so choose different places and activities with this in mind. Include similar settings, e.g. seaside resorts in different seasons, and also unusual ones, e.g. a Tibetan monastery.

The game contains many possible variations of play. Pupils can also use the ideas behind this game in Art, creating their pictures having considered what sounds they wish them to exude.

Game B
Sounds of a Picture

How to play

A selection of pictures are laid out on the table. Each one is labelled with a title. Players select a picture, and have five minutes to make notes.

Players then describe (not mimic) the sounds that might be heard from the picture by the cameraman/artist. They can (and should) include off-camera noises, providing they are appropriate, e.g. 'Buzz of a helicopter' (not appropriate if the scene is set in Ancient Greece).

Each player describes five sounds from the picture. When finished, the pictures are placed face-up on the table. Players write down their memory of the different sounds chosen for each picture (set a time limit for this). Lists are then read out and matched to the players' original records; one point is awarded for every correct recall.

It is interesting to note the varied imaginative skills that are exhibited by different players. Some focus on one aspect, e.g. animal sounds, others display lateral thinking skills and some find it extremely difficult to extend their imagination outside the frame of the picture before them.

For individual pupils, this game can be adapted to involve memory recall spanning a longer period of time. The pupil creates a written description of the sounds within a number of different pictures. Recall is tested a week later, when the pupil is shown pictures, but not the list. This helps to develop study skills that use pictorial mind-maps by encouraging tactics of association and recall. The pupil may decide to support success by identifying sounds in each picture that match a predetermined list, e.g. sound of weather, a vehicle, an appropriate bird, sounds made by people, an animal sound. By observing the different applicational approaches different pupils exhibit, teachers can better see the nature of individual learning styles.

Game B
Sounds of a Picture

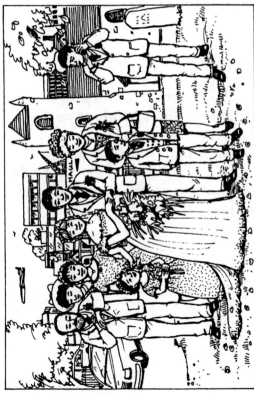

Game C
Cryptic Clues

A game developing thinking and spelling skills

There are some individuals who find cryptic crossword clues impossible to comprehend. However, it is worth investigating your pupils' interest in this game, as I have found that some are absolutely fascinated by the twiddles and riddles that can be created with the English language. This nature of focus also registers spellings in a way that develops memory prompts and long-term memory recall.

Lateral thinking skills are also utilised. As many dyslexics possess good lateral thinking skills, they enjoy this element of play, which allows them the opportunity to develop (and excel) in this type of approach when solving other problems.

There are (variable) conventions of language used in cryptic clues (e.g. I have used capital letters to denote anagrams); this language provides another example of how a communication style can convey meaning.

Preparation

Copy clues for each player. Provide players with an empty crossword grid. Ensure dictionaries, pens and paper are to hand. In some cases, discuss clues together, or provide answers and let players match them to clues.

New crosswords can be created by teachers or pupils, and others found in puzzle books. These can be displayed by hand or through IT.

Introduce the use of anagram-solving books, along with a thesaurus. 'Quick' crosswords and general knowledge ones also help to develop literacy skills.

Incorporate key terminology from the pupils' curriculum, and play about with clues that share a theme (e.g. birds or parts of the body).

Game C
Cryptic Clues

How to play

Working individually, as pairs, or in groups, players attempt to complete the crossword before their opponent(s). Support the players as necessary.

Conventions of play are illustrated in the crossword overleaf. These include:

When last bit of slab is added to road it becomes very <u>wide</u>. (5)

The word(s) underlined indicate a synonym. The solution (broad) is created by the last letter of 'slab' being added to 'road'.

Car in south east will <u>frighten</u> me. (5)

South east = se; The solution (scare) is created by the letters se going around the word car.

Shake A TONIC to create some <u>movement</u>. (6)

Capitalisation indicates an anagram. The solution (action) is created by rearranging the letters of 'a tonic'.

Jan, you and headless Mary join together for a <u>month</u>. (7)

Letters can be denoted by words, you = u; bee = b; etc. The solution (January) is created by adding Jan + u + ary.

Henry arrives before 8. He is <u>1.5 metres tall</u>. (6)

Use words that are often misspelled. The solution (height) is created by putting 'h' before 'eight'.

© Sally Raymond, 2003, 'Dragonfly Games', ISBN 1-84312-038-0. Published by David Fulton Publishers.

Game C
Cryptic Clues

Game C
Cryptic Clues

J	O	I	N	E	D		S	T	A	B	L	E
A		T		A					R			N
N		A	R	R	I	V	E		C	O	P	E
U		L		L		A			A			M
A		Y		Y	E	S	T	E	R	D	A	Y
R						E						
Y	O	U	N	G				A	T	T	I	C
					K							E
A	L	U	M	I	N	I	U	M		U		R
S		N			T			A		N		T
H	E	I	R			H	E	I	G	H	T	A
O		T						I		I		I
P	L	E	A	S	E		S	C	R	E	E	N

© Sally Raymond, 2003, 'Dragonfly Games', ISBN 1-84312-038-0. Published by David Fulton Publishers.

Game C
Cryptic Clues

Letters that are underlined indicate the meaning of the solution.

South east = se; king = k; you = 'u'; Edward = e, Sam = s, etc.

LETTERS IN CAPITALS INDICATE AN ANAGRAM.

e.g. Shake A TONIC to get <u>some movement</u> (6). Solution = ACTION.

Across
1. Jo, Oliver, Ian, Naomi, Emma and Danny are <u>linked together</u>. (6)
4. Sarah sits up to the table to design a <u>home for a horse</u>. (6)
7. The RIVER Avon will <u>get there</u> eventually. (6)
9. Cop takes Edward along to help him <u>handle the situation</u>. (4)
10. <u>Before today</u> is over, I must rearrange mY SEED TRAY. (9)
11. You sing without Sam Iddle to those who are <u>not very old</u>. (5)
12. Initially, Ann tried to install carpet into <u>space under the roof</u>. (5)
15. A plump pin pip pump works when Pat leaves to find <u>shiny metal</u>. (9)
19. Henry Evan Ian Reed is my <u>next of kin</u>. (4)
20. Henry arrives before 8. He is <u>1.5 metres tall</u>. (6)
21. LEAP around the SE to <u>make me happy</u>. (6)
22. Sam, Carl, Ron, Evan, Eddie and Nina <u>hide</u> from sight. (6)

Down
1. Jan, you and headless Mary join together for <u>a month</u>. (7)
2. A damaged TAIL with 25th letter of alphabet is found in <u>a country</u>. (5)
3. We messed up the RELAY and finished <u>too soon</u>. (5)
5. When last bit of slab is added to road it becomes <u>very wide</u>. (5)
6. Eddie, Nina, Evan, Mary and Yasmin are <u>not on his side</u>. (5)
8. Vane turns North to South to make <u>a container for flowers</u>. (4)
13. Edward swops places with you in curtain call, <u>just to be sure</u>. (7)
14. King and headless mite <u>fly up in the sky</u>. (4)
15. <u>A place that sells things</u> for A POSH do. (1.4)
16. UNTIE it and <u>join together</u>. (5)
17. Look inside Magi coats to see if they hide <u>tricks up their sleeve</u>. (5)
18. UNITE them and let them <u>go free</u>. (5)

Game D
Quiz the Numbers

A game investigating the properties of numerical displays

Many dyslexics have difficulties with mathematics. Mathematical instruction involves the understanding and memorising of mathematical language (add, divide, %, ³/₄ etc.), both as linguistic terms and as symbolic representations. Mathematics includes conventions of display (e.g. 17 represents seventeen, not 71); multiplicity of terms (e.g. 'times, multiplication, lots of') and application of memory (e.g. multiplication tables). Mathematical language, symbolic representations and sequential applications are all features the dyslexic may have difficulty assimilating, retaining and recalling with accuracy and speed.

As mathematics is a subject that builds on early and subsequent knowledge, early failings can arrest development, and undermine self-esteem, understanding and success.

Dyscalculia is a specific difficulty with mathematical concepts and application that goes beyond a purely language-based difficulty. In the way that some dyslexic readers fail to extract comprehension from words they can read, dyscalculics lack an ability to associate numbers with meaning, and therefore fail to recognise patterns, appreciate concepts and establish understanding successfully.

Quiz the Numbers is a game that develops familiarity with numerical properties, patterns and displays in a pupil-friendly manner. Questions can be adapted to suit different age groups and needs; larger numbers and decimal placement can be included; and fractions can be used instead of whole numbers.

After the game has been introduced in class, home application provides a valuable opportunity for over-learning and discovery. Pupils can also devise their own questions, developing their appreciation of the wording and display required to achieve clarity of meaning.

Preparation

Cut up a number of coloured card squares and write a digit on each one. Include the digits 0 to 9 with some duplicates. (After use, these cards are put to one side.)

Select a number of questions, according to ability and need, and write them on to larger coloured cards. Allow enough questions (you can include duplicates) for each player to be asked six questions. (The game ends when all cards have been used.)

Game D
Quiz the Numbers

Provide score cards, and play the game alongside pupils, delivering appropriate support and advice where necessary.

The game can then be played outside lessons to over-learn inputs and application.

Game D
Quiz the Numbers

Name:..

Date:.................................Form:................................

Playing instructions

Turn over two numbers.

Decide which number you wish them to display, e.g. 13 or 31.

Then turn over a quiz card.

If your number scores a 'yes' or it can be used to complete a task successfully, score five points.

Game D
Quiz the Numbers

Questions and tasks (select according to need)

Add the number to 237. Is the answer divisible by 3?	Can the number be divided exactly by 10?	Draw a picture that includes both digits.	Tell a story that uses the number 3 times.
Can the number be divided exactly by 5?	Is the number an odd number?	Can the number be divided exactly by 8?	Is it an even number?
Could the number be a date on a calendar?	$\dfrac{number}{2} < 20$?	Can the number be divided exactly by more than 2 numbers?	Is the number multiplied by 10 bigger than 300?
Is the number divided by 10 less than 5?	If your number represents minutes, where would the minute hand appear on a clock?	Subtract the number from 100. Is the answer less than 50?	If your number represents hours, express it in terms of days.
What is the reciprocal of the number?	Is 2 times the number less than 50?	Can the number be divided exactly by 7?	Is 4% of the number less than 2?

Note: Some questions are displayed in words, others use mathematical symbols. Apply these variations to develop decoding skills.

Game E
Syllable Spellings

Breaking words down into syllables appears an easy task, and one that many spellers use to deconstruct long words. However, sometimes you will find that a dyslexic pupil cannot 'hear' the beat of syllabification or recognise where onset and rime breaks appear.

Prefix and suffix recognition may not be established. Chunking 'disappear' into 'di-sa-ppear' is an example of this, whereas 'dis-a-ppear' would indicate recognition of the prefix 'dis'.

'Syllable Spellings' supports learning by identifying the number of syllables to expect from a word. It also allows spelling constructions to be analysed by using words such as 'beauty', 'beautiful' and 'beautifully'. The rules of suffixing (e.g. addition of -ing) can also be practised through words such as 'hop' and 'hopping', and 'hope' and 'hoping'. Spelling oddities should be included, e.g. 'head', 'heading' and 'headless' (over-learning 'head'), and 'collection' and 'admission' involving choices of '-tion' and '-sion'.

An initial bank of words can be extended as proficiency develops. As pupils meet novel terminology elsewhere in their curriculum, this too can be added, along with any words individual players find persistently difficult to spell.

Preparation

Write words of different syllable length on to pieces of different coloured card, writing the number of syllables on the back of each one. Laminate the card for longevity and cut it up into individual words.

Provide a game pathway, with squares randomly numbered 1 to 5, one die, playing pieces for each player and place word cards face-down on the table stacked in piles of shared syllable length. (There are blank game pathways on pp. 73–76.)

Game E
Syllable Spellings

Suggestions for words

1 syllable	2 syllables	3 syllables	4 syllables	5 syllables
school	kindness	beautiful	beautifully	unforgettable
kind	kindly	disappear	disappearing	unforgivable
ice	icy	forgetful	forgivable	electricity
night	frighten	displeasing	disapproving	photosynthesis
fright	pleasure	appearing	February	disapprovingly
please	beauty	icicle	unexciting	unfortunately
give	appear	frightening	exploration	alliteration
	forgive		invitation	

Playing instructions

Move your playing piece according to the throw of a die.

Listen to the word containing an appropriate number of syllables.

Break the word down into syllables, then write it down.

If your spelling is incorrect, go back four squares.

If correct, remain on the square until your next go.

© Sally Raymond, 2003, 'Dragonfly Games', ISBN 1-84312-038-0. Published by David Fulton Publishers.

Game F
Opposite Choices

Word meanings and word association

Reading comprehension difficulties can be caused by word-finding difficulties. The reader might decode the word from text, but there is a specific difficulty in the processing channels that attach the word to the meaning.

Additionally, associated words are primed, e.g. 'cat' should subconsciously prime words such as 'kitten', 'meow' and 'Siamese'. This enables fluidity of speech, predictive hearing and reading comprehension through contextual meaning and expectation.

Pupils who use a lot of ers, y'knows and thingumajigs in their speech may have word-finding difficulties. They often take a long time to take on board novel terminology, confuse words with similar meanings, confuse homophones such as 'whose/who's' and 'road/rode' and struggle to compose interesting text.

'Opposite Choices' provides a single-word reading exercise that focuses on connecting decoding skills to word meanings and associated-word stores (semantic memory).

The game template on p. 22 has already been filled in with words. You can also provide a variety of games using different words, matching them to mainstream curriculum needs. Include words that have more than one meaning and/or opposite, e.g. policeman, which could be opposite to policewoman or criminal, civilian or gendarme. The game can be played solely to support a subject such as second languages or science. Through the assimilation of word meanings and word associations, terminology becomes more readily retrievable. If words can be established in the reading, writing and spoken vocabularies, they stand more chance of remaining there.

Alternatively, provide words that can be paired into familiar phrases (extending word-association links), e.g. 'telephone' (player adds 'box', 'book', 'call', 'line' or 'receiver').

Game F
Opposite Choices

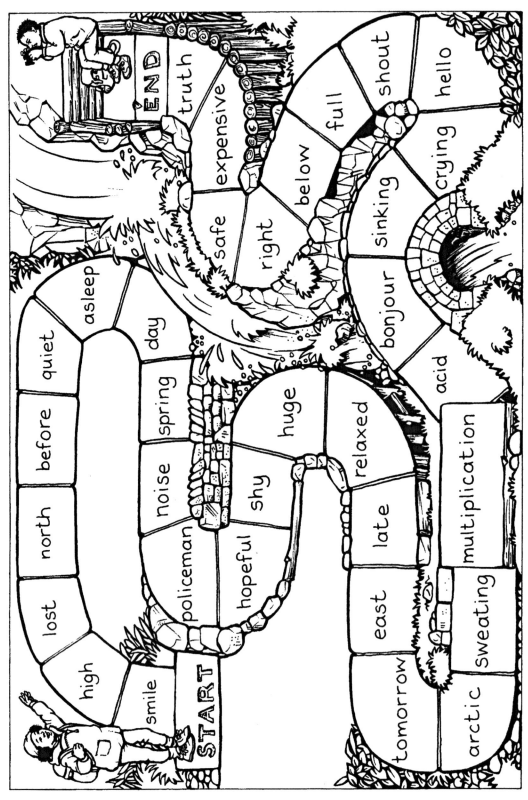

Game F
Opposite Choices

Playing instructions

Throw the die and move your piece along the pathway.

Speak, then write down, a word with an opposite meaning.

If the word has already been 'used' an original opposite must be found.

If no opposite is suggested, the player moves back three spaces.

The first person to reach the end of the pathway wins.

© Sally Raymond, 2003, 'Dragonfly Games', ISBN 1-84312-038-0. Published by David Fulton Publishers.

Game G
Root Word Bingo

Developing spelling and listening skills, along with the ability to identify root words

Everyone enjoys a game of bingo. The uses of this game are endless, but for this version, I have selected root words for the focus of play.

Players have a bingo card displaying a selection of root words. A composite word is read out, and players cross out, or cover, the corresponding root word if it appears on their card.

This game calls on listening skills, and highlights the root word component of many spellings, and word meanings. Players practise single-word reading skills, and are introduced to the game of bingo as an enjoyable learning resource to help them achieve success.

Adaptive possibilities

Identifying the roots of words is just one of many uses bingo can be put to (see **Bingo Opposites; game T**).

Other suggestions are:

- **'Homophone choices'**, e.g. 'rode' on one card, 'road' on another: when one is read out in a meaningful sentence, players have to decide which spelling matches which word.

- **'Parts of proverbs'**, in which words such as 'hand' and 'bush' appear on bingo cards. Proverbs are read out with missing words, e.g. 'A bird in the...is worth two in the bush'. Many dyslexics find proverbs and adages hard to understand. Playing bingo with these phrases allows investigation and discussion to support learning.

- **'Anagram bingo'**. This really makes the mind consider which letters are represented by the key word that is read out. It is not always an easy game, but is an interesting challenge that supports spelling skills.

Game G
Root Word Bingo

Bingo cards

appear	please	oxygen	ice
music	holy	light	event

aware	gram	angle	advise
write	fast	water	count

Root words

Cut these up and place in a pile on the table. Players take it in turns to read root words, or one person is allocated caller for each game.

disappearing	pleasure	dioxide	icicle
musician	holiday	photograph	uneventful
wary	milligram	triangular	unadvisable
written	breakfast	aquatic	unaccountable

Game H
Heads and Tails

Creating words by matching onset and rimes

Studies have shown that dyslexics often chunk words in an inappropriate way, e.g. 'di-sap-po-inted instead of 'dis-a-ppoint-ed'. Playing with onsets and rimes helps to develop appropriate chunking skills that develop spelling and reading ability, e.g. 'sh + op' and 'fl + ight' (the break occurring before a vowel sound).

Heads and Tails is very simple (based on dominoes) but it highlights, and supports, those who over-utilise a whole-word decoding approach rather than identifying familiar letter strings such as 'ight' and 'shr'. By focusing on the components of spellings, in a game, players over-learn and discover sound-to-letter groupings more successfully than when taxed with accompanying contextual reading or writing demands.

Preparation

Copy, laminate and cut up the onsets and rimes overleaf. Add others if you wish, but beware of combinations such as 'ight...cr', 'ap...wh' and, if using a rime such as '-ear', ensure possible matches share the same sound, e.g. 'sp-ear' but not 'w-ear', unless you positively want to draw attention to a choice of pronunciation.

How to play

Lay the cards face down on a table.

Each player picks five cards and places them face-up before them.

Another card is turned over on the table to begin play.

The first player to create a real word, correctly spelled, goes first.

Players take it in turns to add to the line of words.

If unable to go, pick another card.

The first player to use up all their cards is the winner.

Game H
Heads and Tails

ace cr	ip gr	ink pl	own br
ain cr	ush dr	ess pl	ing sh
aying cr	unch dr	ibble pl	ay sh
arp gr	umble st	aying br	ill sh
ift gr	ain st	ate br	ain d

Provide each player with a cardboard shield (or stand an open book up in front of the player's cards) in order to keep the cards out of sight of opponents.

© Sally Raymond, 2003, 'Dragonfly Games', ISBN 1-84312-038-0. Published by David Fulton Publishers.

Game I
Name the Faces

A game developing visual memory

Matching names to faces (and vice versa) can be a challenge for many of us. Name the Faces helps pupils to register salient details and acts as a way of over-learning curriculum inputs, extends the skill of naming topical icons, develops visual focus and exercises the visual-to-semantic neurological pathways.

How to play

Very simply, pupils are given a sheet of faces that they have to put names to. The game can be played by individuals or teams. If appropriate, provide a list of names to which faces must be matched.

Many names have irregular spellings, so this issue can be addressed too; but initially ignore inaccuracies when scoring points.

Players with the highest number of correct answers, or all those with more than three-quarters correct, are the winners.

Preparation

Collect faces from the school curriculum, from the world of fashion, music, television etc. (supporting social skills through knowledge of famous icons) and from members of the school community. Partial displays, e.g. from the nose down, increase the challenge to notice features of gender and individuality.

To develop weak visual skills, introduce pupils to a selection of named faces, with background details given for each one. Remove them from sight. Deliver the faces alone now, or at a later time, and record pupil success.

Game J
The –ing Game

How to play

Players take turns to move their piece along the pathway according to the throw of a die. Having landed on a word, the player writes it down with the addition of -ing. Three outcomes are possible:

- -ing 'eats the e' at the end of the root word (move back one square);

- the terminal consonant is doubled to protect a short vowel from -ing (move forward two squares);

- -ing is just attached to the word (remain on same square).

The first player to reach the end is the winner.

Game J
The –ing Game

The suffixing rules of –ing

Game J
The –ing Game

Adaptive possibilities

Words with different suffixing needs can be used, e.g. words that need to be put into the plural:

• add 's' (remain on same square);

• add '-es' (move forward two squares);

• change root word, e.g. tooth/teeth (move back one square).

Different words might contain a choice of spelling rule, e.g. pictures of words containing 'k/ck/ic':

• 'ck' making a 'k' sound follows 'short' vowel sound, e.g. 'cl<u>o</u>ck';

• 'k' follows other sounds, e.g. 'look' and 'park';

• 'ic' ends words with more than one syllable, in place of 'ck'.

Game J
The –ing Game

Examples of ck/k/ic words presentable through pictures

ck	k	ic
black	bike	magic
rocket	leek	picnic
rucksack/back pack	bark (tree)	attic
duckling	ankle	music
buckle	(elephant's) trunk	public (toilets)
pocket	book	comic
clock	skunk	elastic (band)
wreck	cloak	electric (drill)
bucket	joke...knock...knock	Sonic (the hedgehog)
tick	week	Altantic

Game K
Dicey Spellings

Transferring spellings into long-term memory

This game works by encouraging the brain to store spellings securely while working memory is occupied with another task.

How to play

Write spellings out on to cards.

The player looks at the card and looks at the spelling, noting rules and/or riddles within it.

The spelling is removed out of sight.

The player throws a die.

The player performs the task assigned to the number thrown.

1	Write the word with your eyes closed
2	Spell the word aloud, backwards
3	Write the word with your 'opposite' hand
4	Write the word using bubble-writing
5	Write the word in the air with your finger
6	Write a word with a similar meaning

Game K
Dicey Spellings

Background information

Often, when this game is played for the first time, pupils follow the steps outlined on the previous page and then, having thrown the die and discovered what task they must do, ask 'What was the word?'

This illustrates how quickly information in the working memory can be discarded, particularly when another task is presented. In this case, the exercise of throwing the die and consulting the table can be enough to wipe out all memory of the word, let alone its spelling, observed only a matter of seconds earlier.

Players quickly overcome this problem. Their brains subconsciously identify the need to retain the spelling memory, encouraging that memory trace to become more secure. This also illustrates how methods of learning spellings such as 'look, say, cover, write, check', while they do contain useful elements that support learning, can be completed successfully through the use of the short-term memory, and then promptly forgotten.

Choice of tasks

The tasks presented in Dicey Spellings are varied, and can be adapted to include other activities, such as 'walk around the room, chanting your spelling aloud' and 'write vowels in blue and consonants in red'.

Writing with the eyes closed, and spelling a word backwards, exercise visual memory, encouraging that processing route to support spelling imagery. Some pupils find it immensely difficult to write with their 'wrong' hand, and others do not. Finding a word with a similar meaning requires comprehension skills. This is vital, as it has been shown that the spelling traces of words that lack meaning are difficult to lay down.

Game L
Name that Tune

Developing audio memory

Many dyslexics have audio memory processing weaknesses. They may 'miss' the 'n/m' sounds in words such as 'sprint' or 'shrimp'; they may be unable to retain orally delivered lists or instructions; they may find sequencing difficult, such as where the sounds of 'June, July, August' do not prompt the recall of 'September'. Their letter-to-sound decoding skills may develop more slowly than their peers', along with the development of letter-to-sound creation: it may be there, but not well developed.

Using tunes and sounds to develop these underlying processing skills of audio discrimination, identification and retention delivers an input relieved of other literacy demands. Games encourage participation and focus, and allow teachers to identify areas of weakness more easily.

It may be that sounds can be identified, but not named (word-finding difficulties); it may be that sounds are learnt within a lesson, but forgotten by the next week (poor transference, storage and/or recall between short-term and long-term memories); or similar sounds might be easily confused (poor audio discrimination).

Preparation

A number of different games can be played. Here are three possibilities:

- A tape of different musical snippets: use a variety of music.

- Identical pots containing different objects. Fill each pot with different things (e.g. paperclips, rice, 5 pence pieces, marbles), or fill pots in pairs (players then have to find pairs and identify contents).

- A tape of different sounds, e.g. water from a tap, pasta being put into a pan; a hamster gnawing the bars of its cage; feet wiped on a doormat; flapping paper.

Game L
Name that Tune

How to play

Tapes can be played 'cold' for pupils to identify accordingly. Alternatively, tapes can be presented alongside a list of possible answers, or presented in a different order first (and identified), before the master tape is played directly afterwards, or after a time delay. (Musical tracks can be broken down into instrumental components.)

Sometimes, listening with closed eyes can increase focus. This also applies to the handling and shaking of pots.

Adaptive possibilities

Tape different voices: famous ones and also ones personal to the school.

Tape strangers' voices, and give them names and professions. Play a tape, identifying the voices, then play a master tape of the voices presented in a different order, speaking different words, and measure identification.

Collate a tape of different languages. Can pupils listen, retain and subsequently recognise languages they have not heard before?

Any listening activity that involves the discrimination and identification of sounds exercises audio skills. Activities should also involve a memory element in order to exercise audio memory storage and retrieval processing skills.

Game M
SPATS

A game using short vowel sounds

Preparation

Copy and cut up this template of potential words.

sh__p	sw__m	cr___sh	th__n
c___t	p___n	m___p	v__n
r___d	st___mp	cl___mp	th___nk
tr___nk	s___nd	pl___g	st___m
ch___p	___p	f___n	b____ck
h___nt	j___m	qu___t	t____p

Make a die with the five vowels and SPATS displayed on its faces (you can use corrector fluid and a marker pen to do this).

How to play

Lay the game words (e.g. 'sh___p) face up on the table.

Players take it in turns to throw the vowel die.

If a vowel is thrown, players use it to make a real word, writing in the vowel and placing the completed game card in front of them.

If SPATS is thrown, the player chooses an opponent, who then reads out all the words he or she has collected. The player who threw SPATS can then choose one word to 'steal', and takes it off the opponent.

When all the game words have been used up, the die is thrown once more until a vowel is thrown.

Every word that contains this final vowel scores five points.

All other words score one point.

The player with the highest score is the winner.

Having a bonus vowel encourages players to try to use a range of vowels within their words. When SPATS is thrown, they are listening for vowel sounds not already in their collection.

 **Game N**
13: Unlucky for Some

A game developing number bonds

Developing number bonds increases understanding of numbers and decreases the reliance on finger-counting calculations.

Preparation

Make up number bond cards that display the number bonds of every number between 2 and 12 (36 cards in total).
  For example, 8 would be displayed on five cards as:

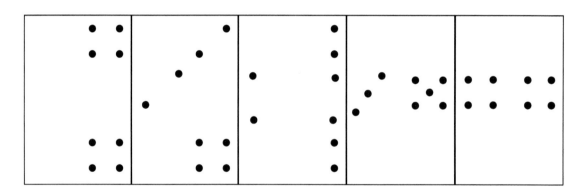

Label the reverse of each card with its number.

Display 11 and 12 on single cards:

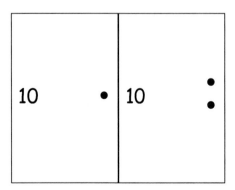

Game N
13: Unlucky for Some

Cut out 12 cards using a different coloured card from that used for the number bond cards. Label these 2 to 13, shuffle them and place them face down in a pile on the table (target number cards).

Put the number bond cards into shuffled piles of each number, with the number upwards, bonds out of sight.

2	3	4	5	6	7	8	9	10	11	12

Piles of cards, number bonds face-down

Pile of 12 target number cards, shuffled and placed face-down on the table

How to play

A player turns over the top target number card (e.g. 5). They then make a guess at which number bond display is on the top card in the number bond pile.

If they guess correctly, they place the number bond card face up in front of them (this also helps them when making subsequent guesses).

If they guess incorrectly, the number bond card is replaced on the top of its pile (encouraging players to remember that bond the next time that number comes up).

If target number card 13 is turned over, the player misses the turn.

The 12 target number cards are reshuffled and the next player takes a turn.

The first player to get 10 number bond cards before them is the winner.

Game O
Similar Meanings

This is a game that develops single-word reading, comprehension and word-finding skills. Word association – where one word prompts the priming of associated words (e.g. 'cow' priming 'milk', 'calf' and 'farm') – affects language-based abilities in a number of ways, such as the delivery of fluid speech, reading comprehension through contextual expectation, listening skills where prediction aids comprehension and writing compositional skills. Dyslexia can cause reduced speed and accuracy of word association, hampering confidence and achievement.

Preparation

When deciding which words to use, consider the following possibilities:

- tangible meanings (e.g. 'house') and less concrete ones (e.g. 'jealousy');

- homophones (e.g. 'through/threw');

- multisyllabic words (e.g. 'disinterested');

- words that are often visually confused (e.g. 'tired/tried');

- adjectives (increases descriptive skills);

- words that encourage lateral thinking (e.g. 'man' could be associated with 'male', 'woman', 'human', 'Mr Brown');

- use words that commonly require alternatives (e.g. 'said') .

How to play

Explain the nature of the exercise by giving examples of word association attached to word meaning. Each player initially moves their playing piece according to the throw of a die, but subsequent moves are determined by the nature of the task and the player's success. Responses should be spoken and then written down, and if a word is landed on more than once in one game, word associations previously attributed to that word cannot be used.

Game template

Words in capital letters require three associated words to be found before the player moves on three spaces.

Words in lower case require only one associated word before the player moves on one space.

Once the player has moved, they wait for their next go before continuing.

© Sally Raymond, 2003, 'Dragonfly Games', ISBN 1-84312-038-0. Published by David Fulton Publishers.

Game O
Similar Meanings

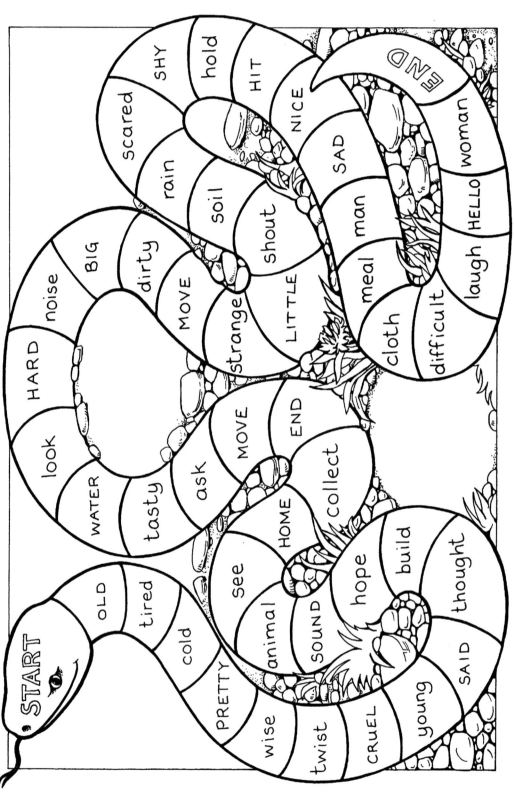

Game P
Adding an Adjective

A game developing descriptive language

Adjectives carry with them both meaning and implication. The 'old man' is less likely to enjoy a disco than a 'young man'; a 'jealous girlfriend' is likely to speak tersely when greeting her 'tardy boyfriend'.

The messages carried by adjectives can be missed by the struggling reader. When writing, the use of an appropriate adjective can both convey meaning and reduce the need for explanatory digression from the plot in hand.

Focusing on adjectives can therefore be very beneficial to dyslexic pupils. It extends their vocabularies and helps them to extract and utilise implication.

How to play

Cards with different characters and locations are placed in a pile, or in a box for random selection. On the reverse of each card are six adjectives that could be used to describe that character.

Players draw up a table (see over) and then each one draws out a card and reads through the six adjectives, with any unknown ones explained, e.g. 'bonny' = 'healthy and cheerful'.

Players then (privately) select an adjective and decide on three physical actions that would suit the character and their situation (no speech).

Responses can by written down and then read aloud and/or acted out.

Players score one point if their opponents can identify which of the six adjectives has been chosen.

Game P
Adding an Adjective

Character	Location	Adjective	Response
baby	in pram	e.g. 'hungry'	e.g. crying, throwing toys out of pram, chewing on fingers
		e.g. 'bonny'	e.g. chubby cheeks, happy gurgling, kicking of legs
medieval woman	at market	e.g. 'destitute'	e.g. begging, scratching with fleas or scratching fleabites, bent over through poor nutrition
		e.g. 'shrewd'	e.g. checking goods carefully, bartering, dismissing sales pitches

Game P
Adding an Adjective

Examples of characters, location and adjectives

Character	Location	Adjective	Response
teenage boy	in park	1 timid 2 lost 3 scared 4 cheeky 5 rude 6 egotistical	Note how similar some of the adjectives are. Players must recognise differences in order correctly to portray salient actions that define them apart.
fairy	in garden	1 belligerent 2 annoyed 3 tired 4 bored 5 inquisitive 6 resourceful	No props are available. If a player wishes to make use of something (e.g. a flower), they must introduce it through acting (e.g. picking and smelling a flower).

Game Q
Scoring Suffixes

A game developing spelling knowledge

This game involves adding suffixes on to root words utilising appropriate spelling rules (e.g. the y to i rule), and scoring points depending on how many real words can be created.

Many spellers assimilate the rules and riddles of English spellings without knowing or remembering many spelling rules. They know 'forgetting' is spelled with double 't', and 'babies' contains an 'i' not a 'y', but many dyslexics struggle to reproduce these displays. They need to learn and understand spelling rules in order to achieve success.

Another difficulty often faced by dyslexics is the breaking down of words into component syllables. This chunking demands audio short-term memory to retain and process strings of sound bites such as 'dis-a-ppear-ance'. With practice, this skill improves, but they can still find chunks such as 'ance' difficult to reproduce. This game focuses on these aspects, providing over-learning and experience to help to develop secure memory traces.

How to play

A selection of root words are written on cards and placed in a box for random selection.

On a larger piece of card, a selection of suffixes is displayed to provide a starting prompt. (Other suffixes can be added as needed.)

Having picked a root word, players discover how many real words they can create using the suffixes, writing a list of their results.

One point is awarded for every word, with an additional point if it is spelled correctly (this latter consideration can be wavered until ability and knowledge are sufficient to justify its application).

Game Q
Scoring Suffixes

Common suffixes

-s	-ing	-ly	-ful
-able	-tion	-less	-ive

Root word: **appear**	appears, appearing (also appearance, appeared); some pupils would also be encouraged to add 'apparently' to their list as an 'odd-bod' spelling
Root word: **vary**	varies, varying, variable, variation (also varied, variety, variability)
Root word: **attend**	attends, attending, attention, attentive, attentively (also attendance, attendant(s), attended)
Root word: **forget**	forgets, forgetting, forgetful, forgettable (also forgetfulness, forgetfully)

© Sally Raymond, 2003, 'Dragonfly Games', ISBN 1-84312-038-0. Published by David Fulton Publishers.

 # Game R
Word Pairs

A single-word reading game (for three or more players)

This game involves reading single words and pairing them with another word (word association), e.g. matching 'emergency' with 'exit'.

How to play

Each player is given a game card displaying eight words.

A selection of other words are placed face-up on the table between players, who then set about selecting words to pair with those on their game card.

By placing an opened book upright in front of each player, they can perform this task without other players seeing their choices.

When all the words are paired, players read out their matches.

If another player has made the same match, e.g. pairing 'birthday' with 'card', players score a point each.

If their choice is unique, no score is achieved.

A choice of pairings is possible, e.g. 'birthday card', birthday present' and 'birthday cake', so players must decide which one they want, and which one their opponents might choose (in order to achieve a score).

By encouraging repetitive play, memory traces for the single words used become established. New cards can be made according to need.

Game R
Word Pairs

Game cards: each game card contains eight words.	Matching words: duplicate twice for four players, three times for seven players etc. Cut up and place face-up on a table.

Game card A

birthday	Christmas (Xmas)	sticky	green
fairy	tooth	car	donkey

Matching words for game A

card	present	cake	card	present	cake
cake	lights	story	lights	park	ride
ride	park	story	brush	paste	jewel
paste	cake	fingers	fingers	lights	jewel

Game R
Word Pairs

Game card B

emergency	laundry	trade	electric
fire	medical	consumer	dentist

Matching words for game B

exit	services	drill	services	room	entrance
services	goods	entrance	services	drill	advice
drill	door	goods	exit	door	drill
research	advice	room	research	advice	services

Memory test

After the game has been played, remove everything from sight. Can players correctly reproduce their game card of eight words?

© Sally Raymond, 2003, 'Dragonfly Games', ISBN 1-84312-038-0. Published by David Fulton Publishers.

Game S
Racing Plurals

Plurals spelled with -es

This game uncovers the '-es' spelling rule by encouraging players to discover for themselves when, and why, it is applied.

How to play

Two players put their playing pieces on to the start grid. By moving their pieces according to the throw of a die, they move around the track. The first player to pass the finish line is the winner.

Players write down the plural of each word they land on.

The general rule is that all the plurals end with '-es' rather than the more widely experienced 's', but why?

During the first round, if a player can correctly identify the reason for '-es', they can add one on to their following throw. Reasons include the word ending with a certain letter (e.g. baby to babies), but in the case of a word such as 'church', it is not the '-h' that indicates the addition of -es, but -ch.

After playing, collate the following diagram, letting pupils list the endings that (usually) prompt the use of '-es'.

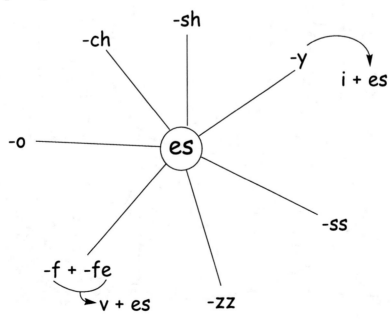

Game S
Racing Plurals

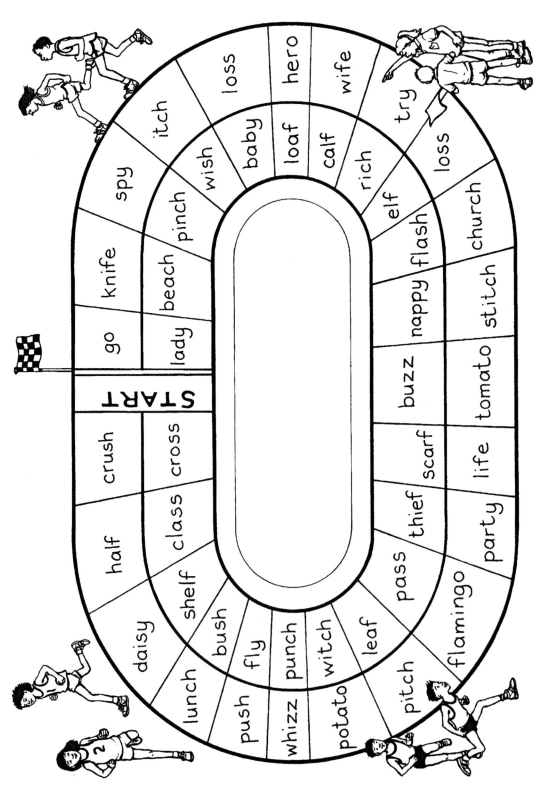

START

itch, loss, hero, wife, spy, wish, baby, loaf, calf, try, pinch, rich, elf, loss, knife, beach, nappy, flash, church, go, lady, buzz, tomato, stitch, crush, cross, scarf, life, class, thief, party, half, pass, flamingo, daisy, shelf, leaf, pitch, lunch, bush, fly, punch, witch, push, whizz, potato

Game T
Bingo: Opposites

Bingo is a useful game for adding some competitive interest to learning.

This version consists of master playing cards displaying eight words, which are then matched and covered with words of an opposite meaning.

This game develops single-word reading, word comprehension and short-term audio memory skills. Once a word has been read out, players must process and store information while they search for a match. Those players that ask for constant repetitions are often those who easily suffer from working-memory overload, which can have a huge impact on classroom learning, so it is worth noting how well players can retain words while playing this game.

Before play begins, ensure that the words on the master card(s) have been correctly decoded, and the possibilities of their meaning understood.

When reading out words with opposite meanings, it can be useful to read them aloud, then put them into a sentence to reinforce meaning. However, this can lead to pupils merely extracting the gist of a word's meaning, and not focusing on the word itself. I therefore prefer to deliver single words, only adding additional support if it is subsequently needed.

Adaptive possibilities

This game can be adapted to suit other mainstream topics, particularly second languages.

Another variation (for three or more players) is to deliver opposite words that prompt players to write down their choice of antonym. Any players who choose the same word score a point.

Game T
Bingo: Opposites

Example templates

Master card A: player 1

impossible	energetic	practical	enlightening
ferocious	pathetic	contradiction	dependable

Master card A: player 2

contemporary	expendable	variable	exude
destitute	gaudy	benign	minute

Opposite words game A (cut up and shuffle)

feasible	lethargic	theoretical	confusing
gentle	strong	agreement	unreliable
outdated	necessary	variable	absorb
affluent	tasteful	malignant	enormous

Game U
Higher and Lower

Supporting numeracy difficulties

Many dyslexics lack confidence when handling mathematical tasks. This can be for a number of reasons.

It may be the language of maths, rather than the concepts, that causes difficulties. On hearing the word 'multiplication' it may take a while for the pupil to recall and identify the meaning behind the word, particularly if they are confused by the alternatives of 'times' and 'lots of'. The language of maths can be very confusing, so care must be taken with all dyslexic pupils to support their need for consolidation and, if necessary, memory prompts.

Mathematics is also highly symbolic. The symbols + and × differ only in their spatial orientation. The symbol % has no salient feature to attach it to its meaning. The symbols of number are meaningless if number-placement knowledge is insecure, and numbers such as 14 (spoken in a reversed manner to others such as 32) can often lead to number reversal. Digit reversal is also common among dyslexics.

Mathematical applications often require sequential application. Many dyslexics have sequence weaknesses.

Some pupils will be dyscalculic, which is a difficulty with numbers beyond the difficulties outlined above. Just as some dyslexics have word-association difficulties (e.g. the word 'lake' not priming associated words such as 'water', 'fish' and 'Michigan'), it appears that dyscalculics lack number-association skills. The number 24 has associations with 2, 12, 4, 6, 8, 48, 240, 23, 25 etc. Dyscalculics find it difficult to assimilate these associations.

Mathematics builds on early knowledge. Pupils who face failure in their early years easily become demotivated and suffer low self-esteem.

Game U
Higher and Lower

How to play

Each player starts off with five lives (e.g. paperclips) and throws three, four or five dice. (Start with three, increasing the number as confidence and ability develop.)

Totals are added up by first looking for number bonds of 10, and then further associations, such as 3 + 3 = 6.

The total is therefore achieved by a reasoned approach that reduces the need for counting individual spots, develops increased awareness of different number bonds and exercises short-term memory skills.

The player then decides whether an opponent should score higher or lower than this total in order not to lose a life, keeping a record of play on a score card.

David		Sarah		
14	H	10	L	David throws 14 and decides Sarah must get a higher score. Sarah loses a life as she did not score over 14. She decides David must get a lower score.
8	L	15	H	David scored lower than 10, so he doesn't lose a life. He decides Sarah must get a lower score. Sarah loses another life etc.
10	L	10	L	David loses a life. Sarah does too. (An equal score is neither higher or lower.)

Players soon discover that there are tactics that can be applied to this game.

© Sally Raymond, 2003, 'Dragonfly Games', ISBN 1-84312-038-0. Published by David Fulton Publishers.

Game V
Treasure Hunt

Developing reading, spelling and numeracy

Treasure hunts are an ideal way of providing short exercises in the form of clues, and carry with them the added bonus of leading around a trail. All players should 'win' something at the end of a trail, as this removes the factor of time, and allows pupils of different abilities to succeed.

Preparation

Begin by selecting eight to ten locations to which each clue will lead.

It is easiest to place one letter at each of these locations, from which to spell a word required to achieve a prize. Players can then be given clues presented in a random order to help to keep hunters apart during the game.

Now write a clue for each location, reproduce them for each player and present each player with a booklet of clues, which they solve sequentially (providing clues in booklets are ordered differently).

A number of trails can be prepared in advance. They might centre on a particular theme, e.g. maths, or utilise curriculum vocabulary and concepts. Outdoor treasure hunts are also good fund-raisers. They can be adapted to suit different ages (including adults!).

The aim is to provide an enjoyable, achievable task. For dyslexic pupils, reading practice, spelling focus and mathematical puzzles are integrated with fun and rewarding purpose.

Pupils can also create their own trails for others to follow.

Game V
Treasure Hunt

Examples of clues

Look under the light lighting teacher's little lattice-work chair. *** Cross out words beginning with 'l'	4 x 6 = 22: fish food pot 26: computer screen 24: paintbrush pot	T o m 's r e d c u p 1 2 3 4 5 6 7 8 9 10 Using the code above, decode this clue: 8, 2, 3, 10, 9, 1, 6, 5. 3, 2, 9, 4, 6.
(under teacher's chair)	(paintbrush pot)	(computer mouse)

Write down the first letter of each answer to solve this clue:
 	
Paris is the capital of . . .
Dublin is in . . .
Madrid is in . . .
The Dutch live in . . .
34 – 14 = . . .
Month after July . . .
Opposite of day . . .
Joint that lets you bend your leg . . .
	reward repap parcs
	
	   ***
	
	Read backwards to find where your next letter lies.
		My first is in gnome but not in monster . . .
		My second's in style but not in yeast . . .
		My third's in worry but not in weary . . .
		My fourth's in climb but not in claim . . .
		My fifth's in queue but not in quit . . .
		   ***
		Solve the riddle to find where the next letter lies.

(fish tank)	(scrap paper drawer)	(globe)

These clues are provided to give ideas of the ways in which solutions can be hidden within clues.

    Different players can be allocated different coloured letters to find, reducing their ability to just watch and follow others.

© Sally Raymond, 2003, 'Dragonfly Games', ISBN 1-84312-038-0. Published by David Fulton Publishers.

Game W
Card Games

Card games are an excellent way of delivering learning. Their repetitive application and opportunity to discover tactics, along with some luck, provide all players with the opportunity to succeed.

However, dyslexic pupils are often reluctant to play games. This can be due to past embarrassment and failure, or purely through a lack of confidence in their ability to learn, and remember, rules of play.

Most games are easiest to learn through playing. Scoring systems and so on should be written down, and rules recapped as necessary.

Fifteens (two players)

A game developing number bonds of 15.

How to play

Remove the kings and queens from a pack of cards. Shuffle the rest. Deal four cards to each player. Place the rest of the pack face-down on the table.

The first player takes one card off the central pack.

They then try and make up a total of 15 using any of the cards in their hand. They can use as many cards as they want to make 15. (Jack = 10.)

If they can make 15, they put those cards into a discard pile, and take one more card from the central pack.

If they can make a second 15, they repeat the process, and so on.

When 15 cannot be made, play moves on to the next player.

Each player starts their turn by picking a card off the central pack.

If the central pack is exhausted, shuffle the discard pile and use as before.

The first player to empty their hand is the winner.

Game W
Card Games

Tricks (two or more players)

Game introducing trumps etc.

Tricks is a simple game that introduces players to the principle of winning tricks without the additional demands surrounding other aspects of play. This means that players can discover the tactics that support (and hinder) success, and gain confidence in their card-playing ability.

How to play

Remove two clubs, two hearts etc. to make the pack divisible by the number of players plus one card. Deal five cards to each player.

The top card of the remaining pack is then turned over and placed to one side. This card determines the trump suit for this game. The card remains on show and is effectively removed from play.

The player to the left of the dealer begins by playing a card of their choice.

Subsequent players (play moves in a clockwise direction) *must* play a card that is of the same suit as the leading card; if they are void in that suit they must either discard a card from another suit or play a card from the suit of trumps.

The winner of the trick is the player who laid the highest card. This card could be the highest trump card, or, if no trumps were laid, the highest card in the suit that was led (ace is higher than king, queen, jack, ten etc.). The trick is put to the side of the winning player.

The winner takes a new card off the central pack (and so do other players), then the winner leads a card of their choice.

The player with the most tricks is the overall winner.

Game W
Card Games

Knock

A simple game involving memory.

How to play

'Knock' has many names and versions of play, but the principle is the same for them all: a player must follow the previously laid card by matching either its suit or its value, e.g. if the six of hearts is played, any six can follow, or any heart card.

   If a player cannot go, they pick up a card from the central pack, and play it if they can. Otherwise, play moves on to the next player.

   However, to make things more interesting, certain cards are attributed with additional meaning:

Ace changes direction of play.	Jack (can be played at any time) changes suit to player's choice.	Eight means the next player misses a go.
Seven means next player picks up a card before having their go.	Two means next player must either play another two, or pick up two cards. If the former, the next player must either play a two or pick up four cards etc. Once someone picks up, the two becomes a normal card.	When a player has one card left in their hand, they must knock on the table. If they forget, before the next player lays a card, they pick up four penalty cards.

   Players start with seven cards each. The top card is turned over to start the game.
   The winner is the first player to empty their hand.

Game W
Card Games

Six times table doubles

This game familiarises players with the products of the six times table.

How to play

Place a list of products on the table for players to consult. Deal seven cards to each player.

Turn over the top card of the remaining pack, and place it beside the pack on the table.

At the beginning of each go, players can pick either a (face-down) card off the top of the pack, or a (face-up) card beside the pack.

After picking up a card, players lay down pairs of cards (face-up on the table before them) that illustrate the products of the six times table (king and queen are wild cards). In each go, they can lay down more than one pair.

When players cannot go, they discard a card (face-up) on the discard pile.

6 = 6	12 = ace + 2	18 = ace + 8	24 = 2 + 4	30 = 3 + ten
36 = 3 + 6	42 = 4 + 2	48 = 4 + 8	54 = 5 + 4	60 = 6 + ten

When one player empties their hand, the game stops. The player with most products laid on the table wins.

This is usually a quick game. Play more than once.

Game X
Dice Games

Dice are cheap and cheerful, coming in all different colours and sizes. It is also relatively easy to find dice with more than six faces, and creating one's own personal dice is an educational experience of its own. (See also Higher and Lower: game U.)

Dice games carry with them an element of chance, which levels the playing field between players of different ages and abilities.

Multiplication square

Very simply, players throw two dice and fill in a multiplication square. Use two pairs of dice for the tables seven to twelve.

x	2	3	4	5	6
2					
3					
4					
5					
6					

Sum sentences

Five dice are thrown in the middle of the table.

Each player writes down as many sum sentences as they can create using the dice, e.g.

4 2 6 3 3

4 + 2 = 6	3 + 3 = 6	6 - 4 = 2	6 - 2 = 4
6 - 3 = 3	2 x 3 = 6	2 x 6 = 3 x 4	6 - 3 - 2 = 4 - 3

Game X
Dice Games

Nines Alive (number bonds of nine)

Rote learning is often difficult for dyslexic pupils. This game focuses on the number bonds of nine, developing familiarity and rapid recognition.

With these number bonds being used as the central theme of this game, there is less chance of working-memory overload reducing the efficacy of memory traces. For example, whereas one pupil may quickly assimilate number bonds through addition and subtraction sum exercises, the dyslexic, who has more difficulty handling the language and symbolic nature of sums, can suffer working-memory overload, one symptom of which is a failure of information becoming established in long-term memory.

Not only do pupils need to know that nine can be split into 5 + 4, 6 + 3 etc., but they also need to associate number bonds immediately, e.g. on seeing 7 + 2, immediately to recognise that they total nine. It is often this immediacy that is lacking in dyslexic profiles, leading to a greater use of finger-counting, which in turn reduces the opportunity of learning through experience and confidence.

How to play

Nines Alive is a simple, quick and competitive game.

Change the numbers on a die from 1–6 to 6, 6, 7, 7, 8, 8 (paint or stickers easily transform dice, or pupils can construct their own dice from thin card).

Use two dice, one numbered 1–6 and the second 6–8.

Players throw the two dice. If they land to expose a number bond of nine, the player achieves a point. The first player to get eight points is the winner.

Game X
Dice Games

Stories by numbers

Write down six associated words and number them 1–6.

horse	foal	tail	jump	stable	saddle
1	2	3	4	5	6

Stories are created, sentence by sentence, using the throw of a die to determine which of the numbered words must be included in each subsequent sentence (the stories must make sense). Note that words such as 'jump' could be used as a verb or a noun.

Either a single die can be used or two dice can be thrown to determine two words that must be crafted meaningfully into each sentence. Stories can be either spoken or written down.

This is not a competitive game, although it can be extended so that players are each given a card of six numbered words (and a die), and create their own stories. Players then read out stories, their opponents scoring a point for every correct 'key word' they identify in each sentence. (This gets easier once words are repeated, and encourages careful listening, helping to develop short-term audio memory skills.)

Follow by number (communal story-telling)

Here players are numbered 1–6.

A story is created with each player adding a sentence, their turns being decided by the throw of a die. Move the story through a beginning, middle and end to direct the pace and thread of the story.

Game Y
Anagram Arrangement

A spelling game (for three or more players)

Dyslexic spelling weaknesses often fall into different categories: those that are caused by an over-reliance on a phonic spelling approach (e.g. 'nite/night'); and those that are based on visual reproductions of a word (e.g. 'nihgt/night'). It is usually possible to identify whether a pupil falls into one of either of these spelling profiles (or both) by making a list of spelling errors taken from a piece of their written work.

Note too if errors are consistent, or whether spelling-error variations occur within the page (e.g. pichur, pitcher, picher, picture).

Of the two spelling approaches, the phonic-based one is preferable, as it is more likely to produce errors a reader can decode. Visual reproduction errors can result in displays that are quite obscure.

Anagram Arrangement requires players to rearrange letters into words. It is useful to pick words that individual players have made errors with in their written work, and to focus on specific spelling patterns within one game.

The competitive element is added by including anagrams that have more than one solution, e.g. 'aple' can be 'leap' and 'pale'.

Players only score a point if one or more of their opponents have written down the same word as they have. This provides a scoring system that is related to spelling luck, not spelling judgement, reducing the negative feedback an alternative scoring system could produce.

Give each player a sheet of eight anagrams. Set a time span for completion. Players mark their results by comparing them to answers provided on a board, and score points according to their opponent's choices.

Game Y
Anagram Arrangement

Example game

teas	recas	resha	ghtlis
e	r	s	s
s	s	h	l
eton	racet	uqtie	atbes
n	t	q	b
t	c	q	b

Solutions

east	races	share	slight
seat	scare (also 'acres' and 'cares', but unlikely to score any points)	hares	lights
note	trace	quite	beats
tone	crate	quiet	beast

Notes for play

Encourage players to apply reasoning to their decoding efforts, supporting the application of thinking skills when solving tasks. For example:

- testing out possible pairings, e.g. 'pl' is more possible that 'ps';
- look out for familiar letter groupings, e.g. 'igh';
- recognise tactics, e.g. the use of 's' to make plurals;
- consider the teacher's approach, e.g. repeated spelling patterns;
- when working within a time limit, move on if you get stuck.

Game Z
Quiz Culture

Reading, writing and general knowledge

Who Wants to Win a Chocolate Eclair?

Integrating popular culture into lessons heightens both motivation and learning. Dyslexic pupils frequently struggle to remember information, isolating them from social interaction with their peers. Providing them with activities that cater for the 'youth of today' not only boosts confidence and awareness of the mobile phone text-messaging and Internet culture, but also highlights spelling needs that these and other genres of culture utilise (e.g. spelling of band 'Mis-teeq').

Studies have shown that while words such as 'parliament' continue to cause errors, words such as 'metatarsal' (the bone David Beckham broke before the 2002 World Cup) are increasingly entering children's spelling vocabulary. By utilising the influence of popular culture, pupils are encouraged to assimilate information in a manner that supports both their social and their academic needs.

Initial input

Players are provided with various media from which to access questions around the theme of 'popular culture'. Decisions must be made in order to attribute the difficulty level of questions, encouraging shared discussions.

Players, therefore, are creating questions they themselves may be asked at a subsequent time. This delivers an initial input of information to the working memory, with a beneficial reward for its successful transference into long-term memory (exercising a skill that is frequently weak in the dyslexic profile). Question cards are created, pooled and put away until the following day or week when the game is played. By approaching the game in this manner, learning (rather than failure) is encouraged, along with preparation and organisational techniques.

Game Z
Quiz Culture

Scoring

A questions very easy	B questions easy	C questions medium	D questions medium to hard
20 points	30 points	40 points	50 points

SCORE CARD

ASK THE AUDIENCE
CONSULT A BOOK
A CLUE OR TWO

RUNNING TOTAL:

Include questions that focus on literacy displays, such as e-mail and website addresses, the language of mobile phone text messaging, product logos and names of popular bands.

Instead of grading questions according to difficulty, you can categorise them into different topics if preferred.

Game Z
Quiz Culture

Preparation

Question cards need to be created that display a question followed by a choice of four answers. Questions must be worded in an unambiguous manner, and the choice of 'false' answers carefully considered.

Question cards need to be labelled (e.g. A1, A2 and so on for easy questions, B1, B2 etc.), and written on different coloured card according to the degree of answering difficulty. Answers are tabulated on a separate sheet.

How to play

Place stacks of different coloured cards face-down on the table.

In order to win a chocolate eclair (or similar prize), players must accumulate 100 points. These points do not have to be scored within one turn of play, i.e. players keep a running total, cashing in their points for a prize when they achieve 100 points.

Play moves clockwise around the table, giving different players turns at being question master and contestant. 'House rules' ensure reading support is given when needed. After the question and choices of answer are read out, the card is passed to the contestant to view. When delivering their answer, they must state clearly that 'my final answer is ...'

Three lifelines are available for each player in each game:

- Ask the audience.

- Consult a book. (Set an appropriate time limit. Any number of books may be consulted in that time.)

- Give me a clue or two.

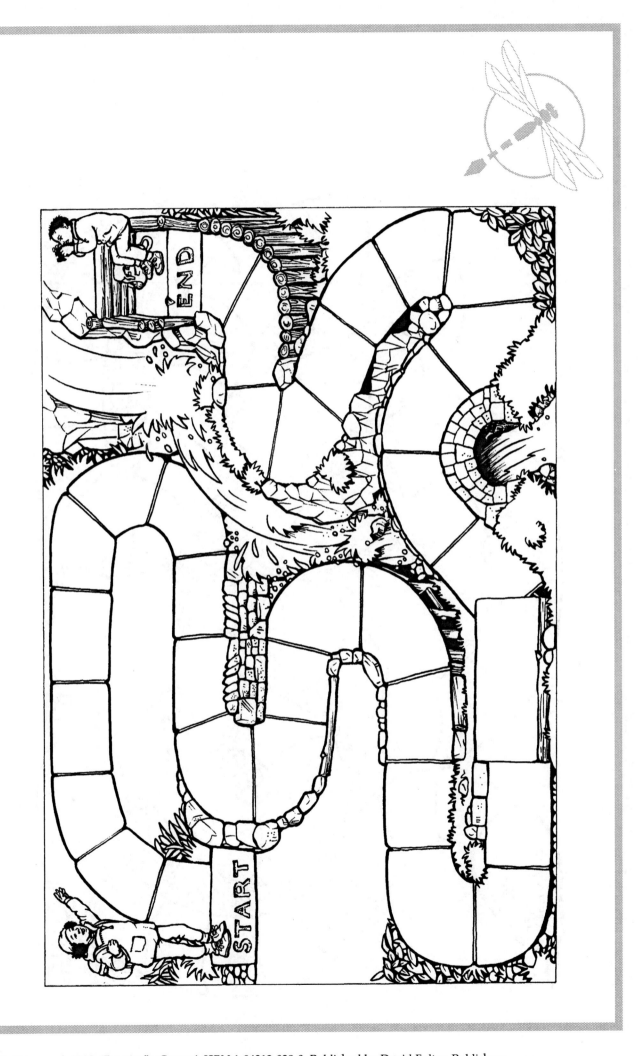

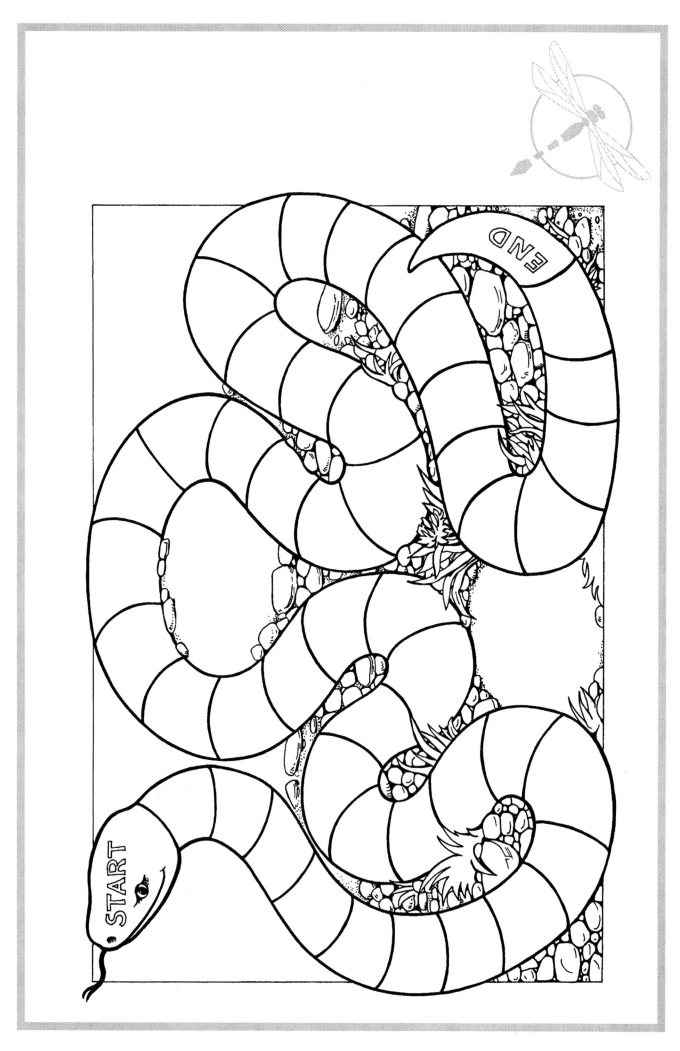

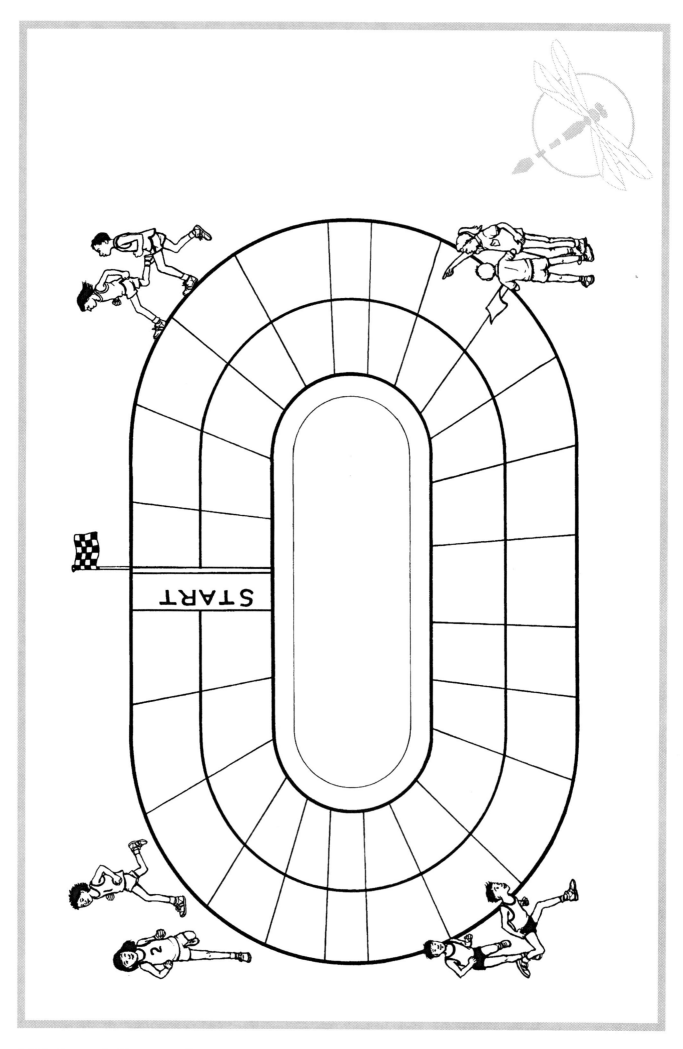

START

Lightning Source UK Ltd.
Milton Keynes UK
UKOW02f1028220514

232110UK00014B/181/P